Tarot

Published by Hinkler Pty Ltd
45–55 Fairchild Street
Heatherton Victoria 3202 Australia
www.hinkler.com

hinkler

Book packager: Tall Tree Ltd
Author: Amanda Hall
Cover and tarot card design and illustration: Rachael Jorgensen

Images © Hinkler Pty Ltd or Shutterstock.com

ISBN: 978 1 4889 4557 1

Printed and bound in China

ELEVATE

Tarot

Amanda Hall

hinkler

CONTENTS

Introduction

Tarot cards have been used for centuries to help guide people and understand the emotional issues influencing their lives. Tarot can bring insight and understanding to personal and professional situations. Working with the Tarot regularly can help you to be aware of changes in your life and to use opportunities for the better. The Tarot is a form of fortune-telling or predicting events. The correct term is divination.

You do not need any special skill to work with the Tarot, but you need to have an open mind and allow the cards to form a story in the way they are laid. A reading of the cards will give answers and advise on how to handle and approach your life. When I perform a reading for a client, I ask them to shuffle the cards on the table to commence the reading. A reading is different for each person, as everyone has unique and varied problems and lessons in their journey of life. The cards work on a very personal and emotional level, tapping into your higher self or subconscious mind. The cards bring out the positive and negative aspects surrounding you.

When I do a reading, I do not ask a question, but allow the cards to describe the answers needed. The Tarot may not always give the answers you expect, but will give you the information needed to look at the issues from an angle you may not have considered. However, you still have free will and are able to control your own thoughts and actions. I believe that forewarned is forearmed and the Tarot can help us make more informed choices to enrich our lives.

History and origin of the Tarot

No one really knows where the Tarot had its origins, but the history of the Tarot cards in Europe seems to date back to the 14th century. The original teaching of the Tarot is said to be based on 22 pewter plates, which made up the Major Arcana. A reading of these was used to decide when to plant crops, or to make decisions for a nation, such as when to go to war.

The Minor Arcana cards were added to the Tarot later. The Minor Arcana consists of 56 cards, which are the basis of the playing deck we use today for card games. In the Minor Arcana we also include four more court cards called the Pages. Images on the cards are used to help understand and perform readings with the Tarot.

There are many myths about the Tarot which have evolved through time. Some believe that your Tarot deck should not be touched by another person. Another myth says that before using your cards you need to sleep with them under your pillow for up to a week, to personally energise them. It has also been said that after wrapping your cards in a purple silk scarf for protection and safe-keeping from evil spirits and unwanted energies, they should be placed in a wooden box and only used on a wooden table.

Tarot is an extremely individual practice and belief that needs to be treated with respect for its ancient wisdom. You should follow your own feelings and desires about how and when you will perform a reading. You can choose a specific place where your personal energy is strongest to perform readings. You might use a particular tablecloth and burn a candle or incense to create a peaceful mood that enhances the experience for you and the person you are performing the reading for. These are personal choices and are not essential to performing a Tarot reading. The main ingredient is a relaxed environment, where you feel at peace with yourself. Allow plenty of time to ponder the message the cards are sharing with you.

Reading the Tarot

Before you begin to do a reading (use your Tarot cards to make predictions), clear your mind of all thoughts. Shuffle the deck, then take the cards from the top of the deck and place them on the table, working from left to right. The Tarot cards all have meanings, and these need to be considered in relation to where they fall in a 'spread' (the place where the cards fall or are positioned during a reading). The position in which a card falls helps give you the message of the Tarot.

When doing a reading you need to choose a significator card. The significator, or querent, is the person you are performing the reading for. The card chosen to represent the significator should be decided by the sex, age, hair and eye colouring of the person. A significator card is used in many Tarot readings as a point of focus or starting point of a reading. For example, if the person you're reading the cards for is a woman over 25 years of age with fair hair and blue eyes, you would choose the Queen of Cups as your significator card. If the female is under 25 years of age you would choose the Page of Cups.

When you begin studying the Tarot, it is advisable to learn the meanings of each card. You need to become familiar with the images and take time to practise.

Later, when you become more experienced, you will be able to use your own intuitive abilities to enhance your readings. Anyone can have a reading, but it is always easier to read for someone who has an open mind and will be receptive to the information being given. People may not always get the answers they expect, and may not want to believe the answers given, but I have never found the cards to be wrong. We still have the right to make our own choices. People still retain the free will to control their destiny.

The cards

The Tarot consists of 78 cards in all. The Major Arcana has 22 cards, numbered from 0 to 21, each with a symbolic image. The cards are said to tell a story – the journey of life – with the figures and symbols representing different characteristics and experiences in life.

The Minor Arcana has 56 cards, divided into four suits – Cups, Wands, Swords and Pentacles. Each suit is numbered from Ace to 10 and also has four court cards – Page, Knight, Queen and King. In the history of the Tarot and other psychic-related subjects, there are unspoken rules and guidelines which have become uniform around the world and have been used for centuries.

The traditional Tarot deck that many people are familiar with is the Rider-Waite Deck, which was first illustrated in the early twentieth century. There are now many other styles of Tarot cards available and you should choose one that you feel comfortable with. In this book we will be using a modern deck and the basic meanings are included on the cards to make them easier to learn. The colour and detail make them a very special set of cards.

Before you work with the Tarot cards you need to protect yourself against the wrong information being given to you by the spirit guides. A spirit guide is chosen to guide and protect you on your earth journey. This may be a family member who has passed over to the other side and who decides to protect and guide you throughout your life. We may not have personally known them before they passed over to the other side. Now we need to learn how to perform psychic protection. Close your eyes and imagine yourself in some form of gold. It could be a triangle, a coat, under a golden shower of rain, in a car or anything meaningful to you. Or you may just like to hold a gold cross in your hand. This only takes a couple of seconds and should be carried out before you commence every reading.

THE SUN.

The Major Arcana

The Major Arcana are the first 22 cards of the deck. They are known as the nouns in the sentence, or the solid part of the reading. They are very powerful in their own right and readings can be done using just these cards.

0 THE FOOL
Good friends. Happiness.
Needing to take a giant leap forward.

1 THE MAGICIAN
Element of surprise. Good or bad.

2 THE HIGH PRIESTESS

Highest card in the Tarot deck. Very powerful.
Good or bad secrets to be revealed.

3 THE EMPRESS

Delays will prove necessary.

4 THE EMPEROR

Stability or stabilising influence coming
into your life.

5 THE HIEROPHANT

Marriage. Government or public company.
Body corporate. Official building or
official situation.

6 THE LOVERS

Love affairs. Romance building again within marriage. Relationship. Relatives. Loving relationship you could share with a friend.

7 THE CHARIOT

Movement of residence. Journey. Victory over a situation or problem. Balancing opposite polarities.

8 STRENGTH

Inner strength. Confrontation with yourself or other people.

9 THE HERMIT

Loneliness. Unattached. Soul-searching time needed or time alone.

Wheel of Fortune

Elevation of money.
Overseas trip.
Completion phases.

10

Justice

Legal situation or document.
Police. Finding out the truth in the
matter affecting the balance.

11

10 WHEEL OF FORTUNE

Elevation of money. Overseas trip.
Completion phases.

11 JUSTICE

Legal situation or document. Police.
Finding out the truth in the matter
affecting the balance.

The Hanged Man

Getting stronger in oneself
after a lot of deliberating and
delaying in your life.

12

Death

Death of situation or endings.
New beginnings.

13

12 THE HANGED MAN

Getting stronger in oneself after a lot of
deliberating and delaying in your life.

13 DEATH

Death of situation or endings.
New beginnings.

14 TEMPERANCE
Money restrictions. Testing the waters.

15 THE DEVIL
Jealousy or trouble. Able to break the chains that are binding you or holding you back.

16 THE TOWER
Catastrophe. Accident. Things happening very quickly, at lightning pace.

17 THE STAR
Brightness. Hope. Could bring excesses, so be careful not to become too greedy.

18 THE MOON

Deception or delays. Emotions up or down.
May be deceiving yourself emotionally,
or others.

19 THE SUN

Marriage. Happiness and bright prospects.

20 JUDGEMENT

Decisions pending finality. The only decision
that can be made under the circumstances.

21 THE WORLD

Overseas trip. Money. Luck. World in the
palm of your hand. New opportunities.

Direct answer spread

Use this spread when you need a direct yes or no answer. The spread spans a three-month period. It uses cards of the Major Arcana only.

Asking your question

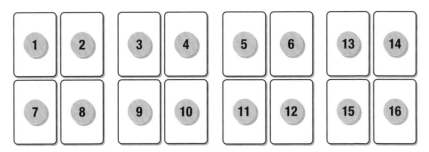

1. Separate the Major Arcana cards from the deck, then shuffle the cards and ask your question out loud.

2. Take the first six cards from the top of the deck and place face up, in a line, across the table from left to right.

3. Turn the deck over and take the next six cards from the bottom and place face up, in a line, across the table directly underneath the first six cards.

4. If there is no conclusive answer, an extension is required. You proceed in the same manner taking the first two cards from the top and the next two from the bottom of the deck. Place them next to the final outcome (cards 5–6–11–12).

Direct answer sample reading

First four cards (1–2–7–8)	Relate to the past, or what is just passing.
Middle four cards (3–4–9–10)	Relate to the present conditions, or the next situation to follow.
Final four cards (5–6–11–12)	Reveal the outcome or to where the situation is leading.
(Cards 13–14–15–16)	**The extension is only used when the answer was not clear.**

QUESTION: Should Mary change her job?

ANSWER:

Past   Present   Future   Extension

PAST

In Mary's past, or what is just passing
The Hanged Man, Strength, Justice, The World

Mary has become a lot stronger after a lot of deliberating and delaying surrounding important issues in her life. She has the inner strength to confront herself and the issues. She now has the strength to face the truth about the issues that have been troubling her and this will bring her life into balance. The world is in the palm of her hand. New opportunities for improvements with money, signing of a contract or new agreements will improve her finances greatly.

PRESENT

The event Mary is facing now
The Sun, The Tower, The Hermit, Wheel of Fortune

Happiness with a lot of bright prospects, even though there has been an end to her marriage. Situations in her life are moving very quickly. Mary has done all her soul-searching and feels she must now move ahead alone with her own opportunities. There have been completion phases in her life and she is moving forward to bring more money into her life.

FUTURE

The events Mary is facing in the future
The Chariot, The Magician, The Moon, Temperance

Mary will be taking a journey which will bring a major victory into her life. Every issue in her life is moving very quickly and there may also be some surprising situations. Emotions at this time will be very mixed with highs and lows, and there will be some money issues to deal with. This may be new territory and Mary is testing the waters in her new direction.

EXTENSION

Extension of Mary's outcome
The Lovers, The Fool, Judgement, The Emperor

Mary is experiencing a lot of loving energy around her at present. With the very strong opportunity for a new romance, she would need to take a giant leap forward with the help of her friends. The decisions Mary is making at the present time are final and the only decisions that could be made under the circumstances. This will bring stability into her life.

The Minor Arcana

The Minor Arcana are the remaining 56 cards in the deck, which can be considered the adjectives in the sentence. These cards give more detail and direction with a reading. The four suits of the Minor Arcana are Cups, Wands, Swords and Pentacles.

There are key words associated with each suit and interpretations associated with each card. Each of the suits is related to one of the houses in a modern deck of playing cards. For example, Cups relate to the Hearts of a modern playing deck.

CUPS (Emotions – Hearts. Water element.)
Cups represent people with blue or grey eyes, and fair to light brown hair. Soft, gentle people.

ACE OF CUPS
Security. Helping hand.

2 OF CUPS
Peace of mind. Joining of two people.

Three of Cups
Celebration.
Bright happenings.

Four of Cups
Money fluctuations. Being
offered something you
may not want.

3 OF CUPS
Celebration. Bright happenings.

4 OF CUPS
Money fluctuations. Being offered
something you may not want.

Five of Cups
Money losses. All is not lost,
if you look behind. You may have
something to salvage.

Six of Cups
Happy house.
Childhood memories.

5 OF CUPS
Money losses. All is not lost, if you look
behind. You may have something to salvage.

6 OF CUPS
Happy house. Childhood memories.

7 OF CUPS

All that glitters is not gold. Look beyond the clouds. Money improvements.

8 OF CUPS

Money problems. Turning your back and walking away, knowing nothing more can be done.

9 OF CUPS

Improvements underway. Feeling smug or pleased.

10 OF CUPS

Happiness. Good things. Party or celebration.

PAGE OF CUPS

Young woman to 25 years.
Basic good news.

KNIGHT OF CUPS

Young man to 25 years. Needing more
confidence.

QUEEN OF CUPS

Woman over 25 years. Blue eyes, fair or
brown hair. Soft, gentle, motherly.

KING OF CUPS

Man over 25 years. Blue eyes, fair or
brown hair. Gentle, emotional, shy.

WANDS (Action – Diamonds. Fire element.)

Wands represent people with green eyes or with flecks of hazel in their eyes, and blonde or red to light brown hair. Positive, motivated people.

ACE OF WANDS

New beginnings. Birth. New ideas. Creation.

2 OF WANDS

Short journey. Movement to or near water.

> Divination is ... looking at the present from a different perspective and seeing connections that were otherwise invisible.

Charbel Tadros

3 OF WANDS

Travel overland. Surveying your kingdom.

4 OF WANDS

Happy home. Possible country setting.

5 OF WANDS

Arguments. Battles around you.

6 OF WANDS

Letter or news coming. Victory news.

7 OF WANDS

Frustrations. You are able to overcome your frustration. You are on top of the situation.

8 OF WANDS

Speedy news or situation coming. Arrows of love.

9 OF WANDS

Undecided. Need to take a step out of the situation. Then you will see more clearly.

10 OF WANDS

Weighed down with problems. Very heavy load.

Page of Wands

Young woman to 25 years.
Travel overland.

Knight of Wands

Young man to 25 years.
Important letter.

PAGE OF WANDS

Young woman to 25 years. Travel overland.

KNIGHT OF WANDS

Young man to 25 years. Important letter.

Queen of Wands

Woman over 25 years.
Green eyes, blonde to red hair.
Positive, fiery, outspoken.

King of Wands

Man over 25 years.
Green eyes, blonde to red hair.
Restless, outspoken, ambitious.

QUEEN OF WANDS

Woman over 25 years. Green eyes, blonde
to red hair. Positive, fiery outspoken.

KING OF WANDS

Man over 25 years. Green eyes, blonde to
red hair. Restless, outspoken, ambitious.

SWORDS (Challenge – Spades. Air element.)

Swords represent people with hazel or brown eyes, and brown hair, or grey or greying hair. People whose opinion we respect: not always older people, but those with a reserved and mature outlook.

ACE OF SWORDS

Frustrations. Double-edged sword. Hollow victory.

2 OF SWORDS

Peace and harmony. Needing to take the blindfold off. Keep reassessing the situation at hand.

Tarot and dreams are two dialects in the language of the soul.

Philippe St Genoux

3 OF SWORDS

Deception. Frustration. Jealousy.
Broken heart.

4 OF SWORDS

Sickness. Bed illness. Needing to
take time out. Rest and relaxation is
needed here.

5 OF SWORDS

Losses. All is not lost as you still have
three swords remaining, giving you the
upper hand.

6 OF SWORDS

Boat or over-water travel. Turning boat
out of troubled waters into calmer waters.

7 OF SWORDS

Plans. Hopes. Wish card. Highest
Minor Arcana.

8 OF SWORDS

Frustrations. Feeling bound and gagged.

9 OF SWORDS

Tears and frustrations. Letting go
of emotions.

10 OF SWORDS

Death or the ending of a situation
or relationship.

Page of Swords

Young woman to 25 years.
Spying or deception. Reflecting
back over your shoulder.

Knight of Swords

Young man to 25 years.
Speedy situation or finish.

PAGE OF SWORDS

Young woman to 25 years. Spying or
deception. Reflecting back over
your shoulder.

KNIGHT OF SWORDS

Young man to 25 years. Speedy situation
or finish.

Queen of Swords

Woman over 25 years.
Brown eyes and brown hair. Cold,
hard, demanding authority.

King of Swords

Man over 25 years.
Brown eyes and brown hair. Cold,
abrasive, demands respect.

QUEEN OF SWORDS

Woman over 25 years. Brown eyes and
brown hair. Cold, hard, demanding authority.

KING OF SWORDS

Man over 25 years. Brown eyes and brown
hair. Cold abrasive, demands respect.

PENTACLES (Money – Clubs. Earth element.)

Pentacles represent people with brown to black eyes, dark brown to black hair and olive to dark skin tone. Professional or business people.

Ace of Pentacles

Money Coming.
Divine wish being granted.

Two of Pentacles

Money confusion. Juggling two
situations or ideas around.

ACE OF PENTACLES

Money coming. Divine wish being granted.

2 OF PENTACLES

Money confusion. Juggling two situations or ideas around.

Tarot helps us look within ourselves to understand our emotions, the reasoning behind our words and conduct, and the source of our conflicts.

Benebell Wen

3 OF PENTACLES

Improvement under way, but delays around it. Renown, glory. Place of worship.

4 OF PENTACLES

Money improvements. More coming your way.

5 OF PENTACLES

Delays around money. Coming in from the cold.

6 OF PENTACLES

Raise in money or salary.

7 OF PENTACLES

Work frustrations. Hard work needing to be done, either at work or a situation in life.

8 OF PENTACLES

Work, paid work.

9 OF PENTACLES

Peace of mind. Contentment.

10 OF PENTACLES

Money contentment. Signing of money agreement.

PAGE OF PENTACLES

Young woman to 25 years. Student.
Male or female.

KNIGHT OF PENTACLES

Young man to 25 years. Visitors.
Message to share.

QUEEN OF PENTACLES

Woman over 25 years. Dark eyes and dark
hair. Professional, business, domineering.

KING OF PENTACLES

Man over 25 years. Dark eyes and dark
hair. Business, arrogant, powerful.

Celtic Cross spread extended

This spread is based on the Celtic Cross, one of the best-known Tarot spreads. The Celtic Cross extended spread can be performed with the Major and Minor Arcana or the Minor Arcana only. It gives approximately a six-month in-depth reading. This spread can be used for a general reading, or it can be used to gain insight and answers to a specific area of your life that needs guidance.

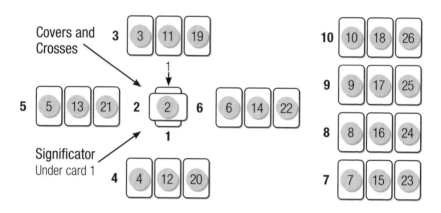

Interpreting the Celtic Cross spread extended

1. Covers the significator, which represents the person you are doing the reading for.
2. Crosses the significator (directly crosses them).
3. Crowns them (on top of them).
4. Below them (influences leaving their life or the next situation to happen).
5. Behind them (influences leaving their life or the next situation to happen).

6. Before or in front of them (the next influence or situation to come into their life).
7. Themself (this is personally around the significator).
8. Home/work.
9. Their hopes or worst fear – which may be holding them back in life.
10. The outcome of the reading.

Sample readings

Bob's Celtic Cross extended reading with Minor Arcana only

Bob is our significator. He is over 25 years old with red hair and hazel eyes. Significator – King of Wands.

Significator

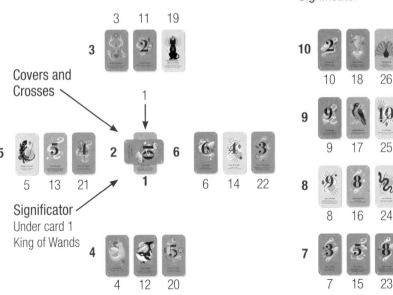

Covers and Crosses

Significator
Under card 1
King of Wands

1 & 2 CARDS 1 AND 2 COVERING AND CROSSING BOB
6 of Swords and 10 of Cups

Bob is turning his boat out of troubled waters. Better days ahead which could lead to a celebration very soon.

3 CARDS 3–11–19 CROWNING BOB
King of Pentacles–2 of Pentacles–Queen of Wands

Our professional businessman, with dark hair, is really juggling a number of issues in his life at the moment, connected to a fiery, outspoken woman, with red or blonde hair. This woman approaches her life with a positive outlook and together they can find an acceptable outcome to the issues at hand.

> The true Tarot is symbolism; it speaks
> no other language and offers no other signs.

A. E. Waite

Ace of Cups
Security. Helping hand.

King of Cups
Man over 25 years.
Blue eyes, fair or brown hair.
Gentle, emotional, shy.

Five of Pentacles
Delays around money.
Coming in from the cold.

4 CARDS 4–12–20 BELOW BOB
Ace of Cups–King of Cups–5 of Pentacles
Offer of a helping hand coming from a soft, gentle man with blonde or light brown hair and blue or grey eyes. There have been a lot of delays in Bob's life, but he feels now is the time to move forward with confidence as he comes in from the cold, and the money starts to flow for his future.

King of Wands

Man over 25 years.
Green eyes, blonde to red hair.
Restless, outspoken, ambitious.

Five of Swords

Losses. All is not lost as you still
have three swords remaining,
giving you the upper hand.

Four of Pentacles

Money improvements.
More coming your way.

5 CARDS 5–13–21 BEHIND BOB

Knight of Wands–5 of Swords–4 of Pentacles

An important letter is coming to Bob that will contain some negative news, but when Bob explores the contents of the letter fully he realises this gives him the upper hand on a number of points raised in the letter or document. The end result will bring money improvements in his life, but he may need to spend some money in order to gain more in the long run.

Six of Cups

Happy house.
Childhood memories.

Four of Wands

Happy home.
Possible country setting.

Three of Pentacles

Improvement under way, but
delays around it. Renown,
glory. Place of worship.

6 CARDS 6–14–22 BEFORE BOB

6 of Cups–4 of Wands–3 of Pentacles

There have been a lot of money fluctuations in Bob's life. Bob has been made an offer, which he feels he will turn down, in relation to a house or property in a country setting. There may need to be some negotiation here and he will then see major improvements underway. However, there may still be some delays in the early stages of the negotiations.

Three of Cups

Celebration.
Bright happenings.

Five of Cups

Money losses. All is not lost.
If you look behind. You may have
something to salvage.

Eight of Cups

Money problems. Turning your back
and walking away, knowing
nothing more can be done.

7 CARDS 7–15–23 YOURSELF (Bob the Significator)

3 of Cups–5 of Cups–8 of Cups

Bob is celebrating the end of his negotiations over the house and money matters
he was previously experiencing. There have been a number of emotional and
financial losses connected to the negotiations. Bob is now able turn his back and
walk away from all of these situations, towards a positive future.

Nine of Wands

Undecided. Need to take a
step out of the situation, then
you will see more clearly.

Eight of Swords

Frustrations.
Feeling bound and gagged.

Ace of Wands

New beginnings. Birth.
New ideas. Creation.

8 CARDS 8–16–24 HOME/WORK FOR BOB

9 of Wands–8 of Swords–Ace of Wands

Bob really needs to take a step out of the situation to clearly see what the next moves may
be in his professional and personal life. The pressure from both areas have caused him to
feel very bound and gagged, which, no doubt, has blocked his energy. He is now able to
walk away from this to a new beginning with a lot of new opportunities for the future.

Nine of Cups
Improvements underway.
Feeling smug or pleased.

King of Swords
Man over 25 years.
Brown eyes and brown hair. Cold,
abrasive, demands respect.

Ten of Wands
Weighed down with problems.
Very heavy load.

9 CARDS 9–17–25 HOPES AND FEARS FOR BOB
9 of Cups–Knight of Swords–10 of Wands

Bob is feeling that improvements are certainly under way in his life. He is charging forward to resolve all the obstacles that are weighing him down. There will be a speedy finish to the matters at hand.

Two of Cups
Peace of mind.
Joining of two people.

Queen of Cups
Woman over 25 years.
Blue eyes, fair or brown hair.
Soft, gentle, motherly.

Ace of Swords
Frustrations.
Double-edged sword.
Hollow victory.

10 CARDS 10–18–26 OUTCOME FOR BOB
2 of Cups–Queen of Cups–Ace of Swords

Bob has peace of mind that his life is certainly improving. He has now commenced the journey of life with a soft, gentle female with blonde/brown hair and blue eyes, who is helping him leave behind the frustrations and money losses of the past and look towards a positive new future.

Bob's Celtic Cross extended reading with Major and Minor Arcana

Bob is our significator. He is over 25 years old with red hair and hazel eyes. Significator – King of Wands.

Significator

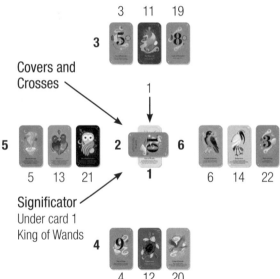

Covers and Crosses

Significator
Under card 1
King of Wands

Nine of Wands

Undecided. Need to take a
step out of the situation, then
you will see more clearly.

Ten of Cups

Happiness. Good things.
Party or celebration.

1 and 2 CARDS 1 AND 2 COVERING AND CROSSING BOB
9 of Wands and 10 of Cups

Bob is very undecided about his next move. He needs to take a step out of the situation so he can see it more clearly. The decisions he has made have been clear and decisive, which will lead to celebrations in his life.

Five of Pentacles

Delays around money.
Coming in from the cold.

The Magician

Element of surprise.
Good or bad.

Eight of Pentacles

Work, paid work.

3 CARDS 3–11–19 CROWNING BOB
5 of Pentacles–The Magician–8 of Pentacles

Bob is experiencing some delays around money at the present time. Nothing is fixed in his life at the moment. The Magician card indicates the element of surprise, so he will need to be ready to make changes and decisions quickly. In the midst of the changes in Bob's personal and professional life there will be increased duties and more work coming his way.

Nine of Cups

Improvements underway. Feeling smug or pleased.

Temperance

Money restrictions. Testing the waters.

King of Swords

Man over 25 years. Brown eyes and brown hair. Cold, abrasive, demands respect.

4 CARDS 4–12–20 BELOW BOB

9 of Cups–Temperance–King of Swords

Bob feels there is excitement in the air with improvements under way in all areas of his life. There have been some testing times with money and financial matters that needed attention – especially with matters connected to a man with brown/grey hair and deep hazel/brown eyes. This man could be very cold and abrasive in his mannerisms, commands respect from those around him.

Queen of Cups

Woman over 25 years. Blue eyes, fair or brown hair. Soft, gentle, motherly.

The Lovers

Love affairs. Romance building again within marriage. Relationship. Relatives. Loving relationship you could share with a friend.

The High Priestess

Highest card in the Tarot deck. Very powerful. Good or bad secrets to be revealed.

5 CARDS 5–13–21 BEHIND BOB

Queen of Cups–The Lovers–The High Priestess

Bob has been fortunate to have a blonde/brown-haired, blue-eyed lady friend in his life, who has been gentle in her approach to helping him through the issues faced in his professional and personal life. This is now leading Bob to look towards her in a different light, as over time he has been falling in love with her. Bob feels there may be a higher force at work to bring this union together for purposes yet to be revealed. With the influence of the highest card, it will be a match made in heaven.

6 CARDS 6–14–22 BEFORE BOB
Knight of Swords–Judgement–3 of Wands

Bob is charging forward with great speed. The decisions he is making are final and the only decisions that can be made under the circumstances. Bob is now spending time surveying his kingdom for the future and what lies ahead.

7 CARDS 7–15–23 YOURSELF (Bob the Significator)
Ace of Pentacles–The Moon–2 of Wands

Money is coming. Bob's divine wish is being granted. There has been a lot of deception around emotional issues connected with his personal and professional life, which has left him feeling very drained. He needs to take a short journey to recharge his batteries.

Knight of Cups
Young man to 25 years.
Needing more confidence.

The Chariot
Movement of residence. Journey.
Victory over a situation or problem.
Balancing opposite polarities.

The Hierophant
Marriage. Government or public
company. Body corporate. Official
building or official situation.

8 CARDS 8–16–24 HOME/WORK FOR BOB
Knight of Cups–The Chariot–The Hierophant

Bob will receive a message or letter that will enable him to be victorious over very
important matters regarding his professional and personal life that have been taking a long.
These matters will now be resolved quickly in Bob's favour, and he will need to sign some
official documents to bring final closure.

Seven of Pentacles
Work frustrations. Hard work
needing to be done, either at
work or a situation in life.

The Hermit
Loneliness. Unattached.
Soul-searching time needed
or time alone.

Wheel of Fortune
Elevation of money.
Overseas trip.
Completion phases.

9 CARDS 9–17–25 HOPES AND FEARS FOR BOB
7 of Pentacles–The Hermit–Wheel of Fortune

Bob has experienced a number of frustrations around his professional and personal life. There
was a period of loneliness and soul-searching about what was the right decision to act on next.
After a period of contemplation the future looks very bright. With The Wheel of Fortune turning in
his favour and with an increase in money, his old way of life finally comes to a close and a new
direction is being cast.

10 CARDS 10–18–26 OUTCOME FOR BOB
The Hanged Man–Justice–Queen of Pentacles

Bob is getting stronger with each passing day. After a lot of deliberating and delaying about his future, he can now proceed with great determination. There is a legal situation that has to be resolved and will involve important documents and legal papers. Bob will engage the services of a professional, dark-haired woman who is very businesslike and can be domineering in her approach to get the results that she requires. She will bring about the truth in the above matters, and finally bring justice and balance into Bob's life at every level.

Tarot doesn't predict the future.
Tarot facilitates it.

Philippe St Genoux

Daily inspiration spread

This is a quick spread using the Major and Minor Arcana that will provide a reading for the next couple of days or weeks.

1. Shuffle the cards.
2. Take 9 cards from the top of the deck.
3. Read the first row, from left to right (1–2–3 cards).
4. Read the second row, from left to right (4–5–6 cards).
5. Then read the third row, from left to right (7–8–9 cards).
6. Read each row vertically (1–4–7 cards, 2–5–8 cards, 3–6–9 cards).
7. Read in a diagonal line, from top left to bottom right (1–5–9 cards).
8. Then read in a diagonal line, from top right to bottom left (3–5–7 cards).
9. The most important card is number 5, in the middle of the spread. This becomes the now card.

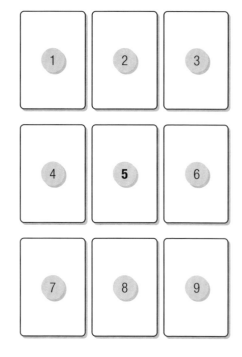

Daily inspiration spread sample reading

Mary's daily inspiration reading

Row 1. 7 of Swords, Ace of Cups, Page of Wands
Row 2. Ace of Wands, Page of Pentacles, Page of Swords
Row 3. 7 of Wands, 8 of Pentacles, The Devil

HORIZONTAL

Mary's hopes and wishes are coming true. She has drawn the highest card in the Minor Arcana. This leads her to emotional security for an important journey she needs to take. The birth of new ideas and creative thinking will lead her to new opportunities that were only pipe-dreams before. Mary will have to learn some new skills. She needs to stop looking back over her shoulder in to the past and focus on the future. Mary is now able to overcome her frustrations of the past and move forward. There is a lot of work ahead of her and she will be able to break the chains that have been holding her back.

VERTICAL

Mary's hopes and wishes are coming true with the birth of new ideas, and creative thinking will lead her to new opportunities that were only pipe-dreams before. She will need to learn some new skills. Mary is able to overcome her problems with the help of friends giving her the emotional support and security she needs. She will need to learn some new work skills. This will lead her to a lot more travel connected with her profession. Mary needs to stop looking back over her past and break free from those chains that were holding her back.

DIAGONAL

Mary's wishes are coming true at great speed. Her determination to learn work skills will help break the chains of the past quicker. This will lead to more exciting opportunities to travel, with her profession always leading her into new and exciting experiences which give her greater skills to overcome the past.

THE NOW CARD

Mary has to learn some new skills and this will enrich and deepen her life.

Seven of Swords

Plans. Hopes. Wish card.
Highest Minor Arcana.

Ace of Cups

Security. Helping hand.

Page of Wands

Young woman to 25 years.
Travel overland.

Ace of Wands

New beginnings. Birth.
New ideas. Creation.

Page of Pentacles

Young woman to 25 years.
Student. Male or female.

Page of Swords

Young woman to 25 years.
Spying or deception. Reflecting
back over your shoulder.

Seven of Wands

Frustrations. You are able to
overcome your frustration.
You are on top of the situation.

Eight of Pentacles

Work. paid work.

The Devil

Jealousy or trouble. Able to break
the chains that are binding you
or holding you back.

Glossary

Court cards: Page, Knight, Queen and King cards in the Minor Arcana.

Deck: Pack or set of cards.

Major Arcana: The 22 cards of the original Tarot.

Minor Arcana: The 56 cards added to the original Tarot cards, including the four different houses or suits – Cups, Wands, Swords and Pentacles.

Querent: The person who is having the reading, or asking the question (see significator).

Significator: The person who is having the reading. Sometimes known as the querent. The card chosen to represent this person is also known as the significator. This is based on sex, age and hair and eye colouring.

Spread: Name given to the various ways in which cards must be laid out for a reading, for example, the Celtic Cross Spread.

Conclusion

I've been asked many times what makes a good Tarot reader. I can only conclude that you need to believe in the knowledge that is being shared with you, and that you should always keep an open mind and remember we all have free will. Life is a journey of learning, sharing and discovery, which leads us to our destiny. I know you will always be amazed by the information given to you by the Tarot cards.

Remember that practice makes perfect. As time goes on, you will find your own unique way of interpreting the cards. Let your intuition develop at its own pace, don't force it. I believe we never stop learning in our lives, so continue to read any information you can about the Tarot because some of this information may be useful to you. Each teacher of Tarot uses different methods and slightly different interpretations. I always suggest to my students that if you like it and it works for you, then adopt it. If not, then let it go.

You will find the more you work with the cards, the more enlightened and enriched your life will become. Enjoy the ancient knowledge and wisdom that is there for all of us to share.